"Parents, read this book to your kids over and over again! These truths cannot be drilled into the human heart too early in life. I'm so grateful Lauren has written this lovely, hopeful book."
SCOTT SAULS, Senior Pastor, Christ Presbyterian Church, Nashville; Author, *Befriend*

"Lauren has taken one of my favorite stories in the Bible and brought it to life."
JAMIE IVEY, Host of *The Happy Hour with Jamie Ivey* podcast

"At a time when our culture has so little to say about death, I am so grateful to Lauren for telling our children that Jesus has all the answers to our questions."
ED DREW, Founder, Faith in Kids

"In this winsome little book, Lauren Chandler applies resurrection reality to the heart, in a way that will help both adults and kids face death with faith and hope."
NANCY GUTHRIE, Author, *What Every Child Should Know About Prayer*

"Made my heart leap and brought me to joyful tears! No matter what season you or your family find yourself in, this book will speak directly to your heart."
RACHEL JOY, Founder and Director, The Sparrow Conference

"A beautifully helpful reminder that, even though it feels like it, death doesn't have to be a forever goodbye, because Jesus came to end goodbyes."
KRISTIE ANYABWILE, Author and Bible teacher

"How do we help our children get over the fear of death? Lauren's engaging account of Jesus and Lazarus speaks profound biblical truth into this common childhood fear. Every generation can read it and be glad!"
BARBARA REAOCH, Author, *A Better Than Anything Christmas*

"Full of faith, beauty, hope, and life."
CHRISTINE CAINE, Founder, A21 and Propel Women

"Such a sweet story, highlighting the merciful heart and resurrection power of Jesus."
CHRISTY NOCKELS, Singer and Songwriter

Goodbye to Goodbyes
© Lauren Chandler / Catalina Echeverri 2019. Reprinted 2019, 2021, 2022, 2023.

Illustrated by Catalina Echeverri | Design & Art Direction by André Parker

"The Good Book For Children" is an imprint of The Good Book Company Ltd.
thegoodbook.com | thegoodbook.co.uk
thegoodbook.com.au | thegoodbook.co.nz | thegoodbook.co.in

ISBN: 9781784983772 | JOB-007356 | Printed in India

thegoodbook
for children

WRITTEN BY:
LAUREN CHANDLER

ILLUSTRATED BY:
CATALINA ECHEVERRI

Goodbye

to
GOODBYES

In the little town of Bethany,
there lived a man named Lazarus.

He had two sisters, Mary and Martha.

Martha loved to
throw a party.

Mary loved to sit
and listen.

Lazarus loved his
two sisters.

And they were all
friends with a man
named Jesus.

But one day,
Lazarus got sick.

He went to bed sick.
And he woke up sick.

Martha and Mary
looked after him,
but Lazarus got worse
and worse...

"I Know," said Martha, "I will tell our friend Jesus! He can help!"

Martha thought about all Jesus had done.

He made the blind people see.

He made the deaf people hear.

He made people who had been sick walk, jump, run, and leap for joy.

He could make Lazarus well!

So she and Mary
sent a message
to Jesus:

Lord Jesus,
    Our brother Lazarus,
    the friend that you love,
    is sick.
        Come quickly!

It took two days for Martha's message to reach Jesus.

And when Jesus heard his friend was very, very sick, he...

... did nothing.

Did nothing?! That's right.

He didn't ride the first donkey to Bethany.

He didn't run until his side hurt.

For two whole days, he stayed right where he was.

Why?

Jesus told his disciples,

"Our friend Lazarus is very sick.
But this illness won't end with Lazarus
being dead. We won't have to say
goodbye forever. I have a plan."

Phew! Jesus had a plan!
But... what was it?

Then, at last, Jesus and his disciples headed to Bethany.

"Our friend Lazarus has fallen asleep," Jesus announced, "but I'm on my way to wake him up!"

The disciples looked at each other.

Did they hear him right? Lazarus was sleeping?

Couldn't Mary and Martha wake him up?

Jesus knew their questions.
He looked at them and said,

Lazarus
has died.

Dead?! How could this be?
Didn't Jesus say that Lazarus would not die?
Didn't he say they wouldn't have to say goodbye forever?

What happened to his plan?

Every step to Bethany felt heavier and heavier.
Their hearts sank deeper and deeper.

They were sad their friend had died.
They didn't even get to say goodbye.

Four days after Lazarus had died,
Jesus and his disciples finally arrived.

Martha came running to meet them.

Her face was sad.
Her eyes were red.

"Lord!" she gasped. "If only you had been here, Lazarus would not have died. But I know nothing is impossible with you—even after someone's died and we've said our forever goodbyes."

"You're right, Martha," Jesus said. "There is a day coming when we will say goodbye to saying goodbyes forever.

Do you believe that?"

Martha nodded. "Yes! I believe in you, Jesus! I Know you are the Son of God. And I Know you always do what you promise. You will end all our goodbyes. Forever."

Martha went and fetched Mary.

Mary was
so sad.

The brother she loved was gone. She would
never hug him again. She would never eat with
him again. She would never see his face again.

Jesus saw her tears.
 And then it happened.
His heart broke.

He knew what he was about to do.
He knew Lazarus's goodbye wasn't forever.
But his heart broke for his friends.

When they reached Lazarus's
tomb, Jesus cried too.

They cried,

    and cried,

        and cried,

because they'd had to say
a forever goodbye.

Martha told him there might be a
horrible smell.

Jesus said, "You need to believe me."

So they took away the stone.

Then he yelled,
like a lion's mighty roar,

"Lazarus, come out!"

And...
he...

... did!

Jesus kept his word.
Lazarus being sick didn't end with him being dead.
It ended with him alive even after he died — after
they'd had to say goodbye!

Mary, Martha, Lazarus, and Jesus
were together again.

Martha threw a party.
Mary laughed and listened.
Lazarus was glad to be alive!

But then the time came
for Jesus to say goodbye.

He hugged the friends that
he loved and said,
"Goodbye for now — but
not forever."

Jesus had to go to Jerusalem,
where he would be the one to say goodbye and die—
and then, like Lazarus, walk out of a tomb alive.

And after that, Jesus said goodbye again,
because he was going back to heaven.

It was sad for Jesus's friends to say goodbye,
   but they would see him again,
   in the land that lay after their dying,
   in the land where there are no more goodbyes—
                                        not ever.

We all have to say goodbye sometimes.

Some of them are short goodbyes.

Some are long.

Sometimes, a friend of Jesus who we love gets sick, and we're sad.

Sometimes, because they die, we have to say goodbye. It feels like a forever goodbye.

Jesus knows it is sad to say goodbye.

So Jesus came to end goodbyes.

And one day, Jesus and all his friends
will say goodbye to goodbyes —

forever!

HOW DO WE KNOW ABOUT GOODBYE TO GOODBYES?

The curious and spectacular story of Lazarus, his sisters, and their friend Jesus can be found in John's Gospel, chapter 11, verses 1-44. It is the last of seven miracles John writes about in his account of Jesus' life on earth.

The interaction between Jesus and his friends in this true story is especially dear to our family. We are very acquainted with illness and the possibility of saying goodbye for what may feel like forever. We have asked Jesus "why" in the midst of our pain. We have questioned his methods but have been comforted by his heart.

He weeps with those who weep. He rejoices with those who rejoice.
He is the God who is with us in our sorrow and our joy.

Although our family's story hasn't ended in a goodbye, it will one day. But it won't be forever. For those who have believed Jesus to be their only hope, physical death will mean immediate presence with him (Philippians 1 v 21-23). For those who are left behind, there is still hope — hope in the life to come, and hope that Jesus will be with us "always, to the end of the age"
(Matthew 28 v 20).

Enjoy all of the award-winning
"Tales That Tell The Truth" series: